How to Create a Teacher's Guide for Your Middle-Grade Book

A Stargazer Quick Guide

Carol J. Amato

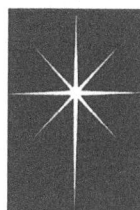

STARGAZER
Publishing Company
PO Box 77002
Corona, CA 92877-0100
"Educate, Enlighten, Empower"

www.stargazerpub.com

STARGAZER
QUICK
GUIDES

Published by Stargazer Publishing Company
PO Box 77002
Corona, CA 92877-0100
(800) 606-7895
(951) 898-4619
FAX (951) 898-4633
Corporate email: stargazer@stargazerpub.com
Orders email: orders@stargazerpub.com
www.stargazerpub.com
www.phantomhunters.com

Cover design: Michael D. Wheary
                     www.calypsoconcepts.com

ISBN: 9781933277257 (Paper)

Table of Contents

Table of Contents, Cont'd.

Introduction

If you're like most writers, you want to increase sales potential for your work. A terrific way to make your fiction or nonfiction book more saleable is to create a teacher's guide. In addition, if yours covers a complete unit of material, it will make your story more useful not only to teachers and home-school parents but also to school librarians. This book shows you how to create a teacher's guide for grades 4-6.

Any topic can lend itself to classroom use. Elements to consider for the guide are the:

- contents
- educational standards
- production method

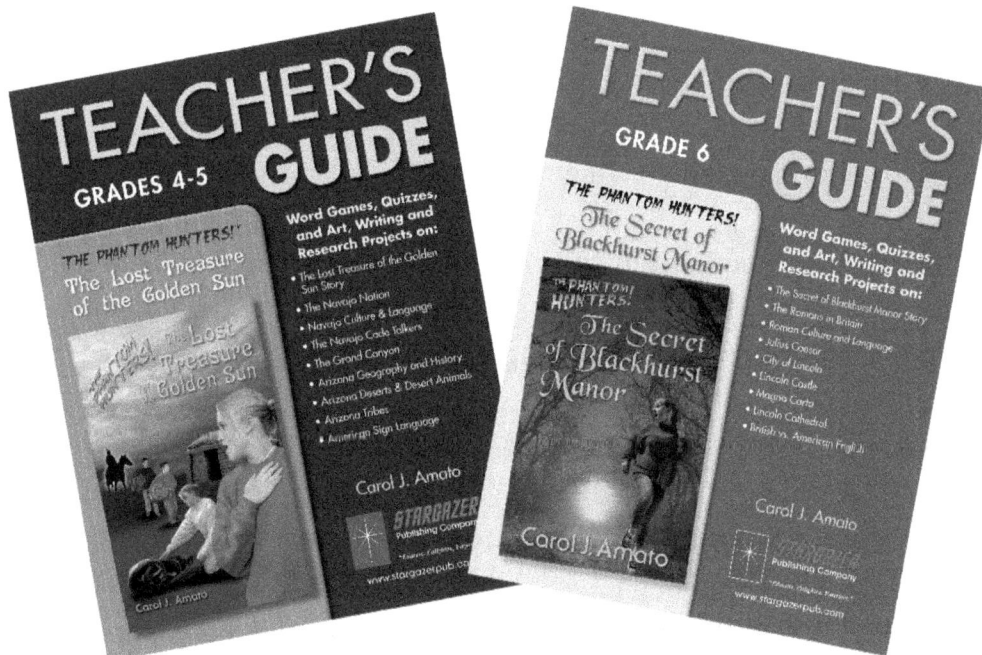

Contents

W hat goes into a teacher's guide for middle grades? Here are some ideas:

☑ Inside title page

☑ Page with the following:

- a note to the teachers and parents letting them know which pages are reproducible (can be copied and handed out to the students)

- copyright notice

- any required permissions for images from other sources

☑ Table of Contents

☑ Two-page spread containing the book summary (for fiction only)

☑ Quizzes on the book

☑ Crossword puzzles

☑ Recipes for food eaten in the context or geographic area of the story

☑ Word searches and matching games

☑ Art, science, research, writing, and math projects

☑ Information about the locale, residents, tourist sites, etc.

☑ URLs for additional research

☑ Answer key for any puzzles and quizzes

The Lost Treasure of the Golden Sun is the first book in my middle-grade mystery series, *The Phantom Hunters*, and takes place on the Navajo Nation in Arizona. That locale lends itself to all kinds of activities and research papers on the following:

- ✓ The Grand Canyon

- ✓ The Petrified Forest

- ✓ The Navajo Nation

- ✓ Navajo culture and language (art, music, folklore)

- ✓ The Code Talkers

- ✓ The *Navajo Times* newspaper

- ✓ Other tribes in Arizona (Apaches and Hopis)

- ✓ Window Rock, the Navajo Nation capital

- ✓ Arizona geography, history, plant life, deserts, and desert animals

- ✓ The Long Walk

I've also included the American Sign Language alphabet and numbers from 1 to 10 since one of my characters is deaf. The topics in your guide do not necessarily have to be limited to your book's content. Here are some examples

Fiction

Let's say your story takes place in or your work concerns Pennsylvania. What

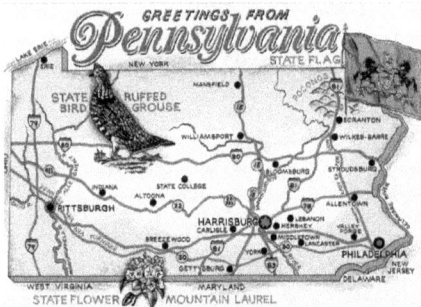

appropriate activities can you develop? How about the Amish in Lancaster County? Or consider the coal-mining regions, Philadelphia history, the history of the area in which your story takes place, and any other interesting landmarks and historical events. These are all sources you can tap for your teacher's guide.

Biography

What if your book is a biography about a famous person? Many of the same topics that appear above apply. Develop activities about the historical events that occurred during that person's life, the region and state where he/she lived, the culture at the time, and so on.

General Nonfiction

Or maybe your book is about whales. Create research projects and activities

aro‼ und that topic. The seven types (Killer, Humpback, Blue, Orca, Beluga, Fin, and Sperm), the food they eat, their migration patterns, and the areas of the ocean they inhabit are just a few. You can also branch off into ocean pollution and the danger it poses to the whales, the problems of keeping

whales in captivity in aquariums, and the realities of the space a whale needs

Using Educational Standards

What activities should you develop for your guide if you are not a teacher? The Educational Common Core Standards (ECCS) and state educational standards can do the work for you.

What are educational standards?

They specify what students at a particular grade level need to know. They "encourage the highest achievement of every student, by defining the knowledge, concepts, and skills that students should acquire at each grade level" (**cde.ca.gov/be/st/ss/**). Teachers use these to formulate their lesson plans. You can, too.

Educational Common Core Standards (ECCS)

As of this writing, the Educational Common Core Standards (LCCS) "establish clear, consistent guidelines for what every student should know and be able to do in math and English language arts from kindergarten through 12th grade" (corestandards.org/what-parents-should-know/)have been adopted by all 50 states for English and Math. Criticism had been that states had different standards for these subjects, which left students in some states getting a high level of education in these areas while students in other states received a much lower level. The ECCS ensure all students meet the same standard.

State Standards

Each state has its own standards for every other subject. Students must cover specific information for each. You can access your state's standards from the ECCS website.

Make Things Easy for Yourself

The easiest way to use the standards is to gear your book and guide for the grade level and age group of the material in question. Do your homework. Know that grade level in and out. For example, students in Arizona study their state in the 4th grade; students in California study Arizona in 5th grade. I aimed the teacher's guide for the *Lost Treasure of the Golden Sun* to grades 4-5. In California, students study ancient Rome in the 6th grade. The next book, *The Secret of Blackhurst Manor* (due out in January, 2017) takes place in England in a town originally built by the Romans, and some of the characters are ghosts of Roman soldiers. The Romans in Britain is something that isn't covered too often, so here was a chance for me to expand on that. The teacher's guide has to be geared for the 6th grade, since grades 4 and 5 won't be studying this material.

Ancient Rome is included in the California state standards for 6th grade "World History and Geography: Ancient Civilizations" **cde.ca.gov/be/st/ss/ documents/histsocscistnd.pdf)**. The points in the California standards for World History and Geography: Ancient Civilizations are shown on the next page.

Select the Standards that Apply

Standards 5, 6, and 7 don't apply to my guide because they don't relate to the Romans in Britain; however, they might be useful if you are marketing to Christian schools and home-school parents since they concern the growth of Christianity throughout Europe. These standards could be a teacher's guide in and of themselves.

I included activities on Julius Caesar, since he lived and worked as a silversmith in Britain (Nos. 1 and 4), and some on No. 3. I incorporated activities on trade routes through Europe to Britain and on Roman roads. For No. 8, there are many British cities originally built by the Romans and where ruins from that period still exist.

6.7 Students analyze the geographic, political, economic, religious, and social structures during the development of Rome.

1. Identify the location and describe the rise of the Roman Republic, including the importance of such mythical and historical figures as Aeneas, Romulus and Remus, Cincinnatus, Julius Caesar, and Cicero.

2. Describe the government of the Roman Republic and its significance (e.g., written constitution and tripartite government, checks and balances, civic duty).

3. Identify the location of and the political and geographic reasons for the growth of Roman territories and expansion of the empire, including how the empire fostered economic growth through the use of currency and trade routes.

4. Discuss the influence of Julius Caesar and Augustus in Rome's transition from republic to empire.

5. Trace the migration of Jews around the Mediterranean region and the effects of their conflict with the Romans, including the Romans' restrictions on their right to live in Jerusalem.

6. Note the origins of Christianity in the Jewish Mediterranean prophecies, the life and teachings of Jesus of Nazareth as described in the New Testament and the contribution of St. Paul the Apostle to the definition and spread of Christian beliefs (e.g., the belief in the Trinity, resurrection, salvation).

7. Describe the circumstances that led to the spread of Christianity in Europe and other Roman territories.

8. Discuss the legacies of Roman art and architecture, technology and science, literature, language, and law.

In addition, Hadrian's Wall, finished in 128 C.E., still divides England from Scotland. I created a page of words that are the same in English as they were in Latin (such as bonus, forum, stadium, memorandum, agenda, and census). I included word games, crossword puzzles, quizzes, and research projects for all of the standards. Nos. 4 and 8 can be research projects almost exactly as worded.

Create Activities Across the Curriculum

Creating activities across the curriculum means including math, science, social studies, writing, geography, visual/fine arts, history, reading comprehension, technology, and physical education/health. A math activity in the *Lost Treasure of the Golden Sun Teacher's Guide* required the kids to calculate the distance between their homes and the Navajo Nation. If you include plant life, the students can determine the amount of water to feed specific ones, measure their growth each day, write about the uses of plants for medicine and food, how to recognize poisonous ones, and so on.

Combine Curriculum into One Activity

You can combine curriculum into one activity. For example, let's say the students are to write a report on Julius Caesar and his influence on the development of the Roman Empire. They must research on the Internet and include their sources. This incorporates writing, reading comprehension, history, and technology.

To make your activity development easier if you aren't a teacher, think about teaming up with one from your local school. Be sure he/she teaches at the grade level appropriate to your material. If you can't find one to partner with, see if a teacher is willing to review your guide once you have several activities developed.

If your book is really state-specific, as is *The Lost Treasure of the Golden Sun*, as mentioned, check that state's standards at **www.corestandards.org/**.

Production Method

If you are self-publishing your book, you have free rein to design your teacher's guide the way you want. If you are publishing traditionally, however, you will have to check with your editor to see whether or not the publisher is interested in publishing the guide. With luck, they will consider the added bonus of a teacher's guide to be a great marketing tool and decide to produce it. If so, they may either commission you to write it or hire someone else to do so. If the publisher is not interested, ask permission to do so on your own. You can easily create a PDF file and sell it on your website and or post it to Teachers Pay Teachers (teacherspayteachers.com). This way, there is no production cost—at least for the guide interior.

You can also post individual activities on Pinterest for free, but teachers love getting material that covers a whole unit, so if you post on Pinterest, let them know that the whole guide is available and where.

NOTE: *An e-book is not an option because it is not printable.*

There are several things to consider:

- PDF vs. physical book
- Determine the number of pages
- Make your pages teacher and kid-friendly
- Use a page layout program
- What to include

PDF vs. Physical Book

Generating a teacher's guide as a PDF rather than a softcover book has several advantages:

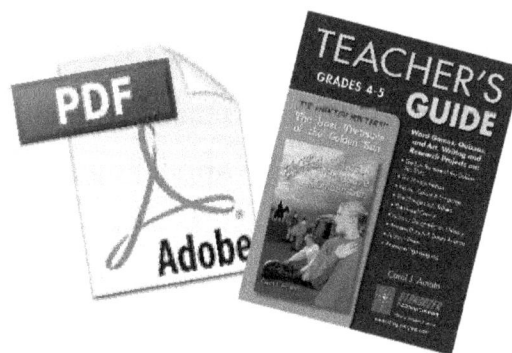

1. Teachers and home-school parents expect to reproduce the pages (referred to as "consumables") so they can be handed out to students.

A printed book requires them to photocopy the pages. That means a trip to the school office or the copy shop. With a PDF, they can print directly from their classroom or home computers.

2. Printed books are expensive, even if the page count is low. A PDF will cost you nothing but your time to produce and the cost of designing a cover. If you sell it, the investment is low and all the income is profit.

3. If you need to update, correct, or add anything to your teacher's guide, you are not stuck with a pile of unsold books that don't have those changes. You can update the file whenever you want and just place it on your website or wherever it's being sold.

4. Your pages can include color images or text. To be economical, a soft-cover book has to be printed in black and white.

Decide on the Number of Pages

If your publisher is producing your teacher's guide or you want to offset-print a softcover book, you will have to make it 32, 64, or 96 pages, depending on the grade level. The count is not an issue with a print-on-demand book or PDF download. You can have any number, but stick close to these traditional guidelines.

Make Your Pages Teacher- and Kid-Friendly

Once you have your activities outlined, it's time to design the pages. They should be visually appealing and include the information that teachers need. Study the layouts of teacher's guides in the book and teacher-supply stores. You want yours to look professionally produced and not like it came off a word processing program or your phone.

Consider the number of graphics versus text, the white space allowed, and how the graphics are used. Teachers will reject a guide with pages that look too dense. Pages with lots of white space look user-friendly.

Use a Page Layout Program

Because a typical teacher's guide includes many graphics, use a program that allows easy manipulation of the elements on a page. MS Word 2010 or above can suffice but is not a page layout program; it's a word processor. You may get frustrated keeping the artwork where you want it. While InDesign is the industry standard as of this writing, it is high end and requires a big learning curve. A user-friendly alternative is MS Publisher. Use graphics that match the theme of your guide. Include lines for the child's name and the date on the handout pages.

What to Include

The pages should incorporate the information that teachers need. As said before, any page that is meant to be handed out should display the word "Reproducible." This tells teachers that they can make copies without any copyright violation. If all pages are reproducible, state that on the copyright page. Otherwise, the best location for this information is someplace in the footer in small type.

Include activities for at least three ability levels: On Level (formerly "Mainstream"), Challenge (formerly "Gifted"), Extra Support (formerly "Resource"), snd English-Language Learner. Develop a code, such as OL, C ES, and ELL for the On Level, Challenge, Extra Support, and English-Language Learner pages and include that, too. Doing so tells the teacher at a glance to which groups of students the activity is geared. Another thing to incorporate is the actual standard(s) to which this activity corresponds so the teacher doesn't have to hunt through a separate page to figure out which ones apply.

Your footer could look something like this:

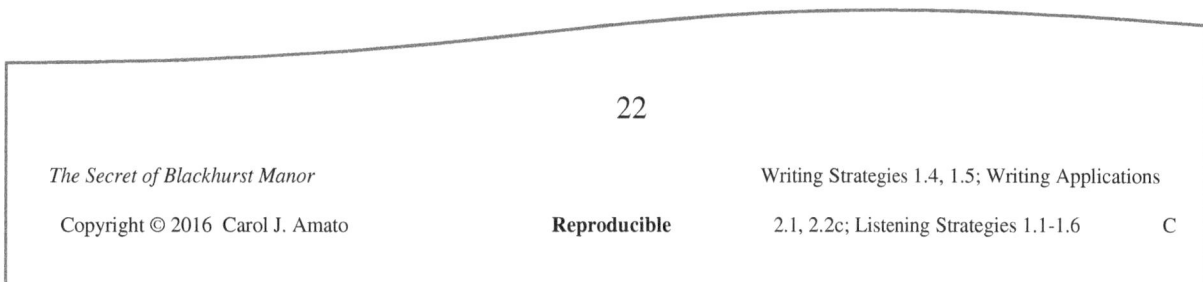

22

The Secret of Blackhurst Manor   Writing Strategies 1.4, 1.5; Writing Applications

Copyright © 2016 Carol J. Amato   **Reproducible**   2.1, 2.2c; Listening Strategies 1.1-1.6   C

Ensure that your pages have a uniform look. Use a kid-friendly font for the text and a different, larger font for the headings. In addition, give your activities kid-friendly titles.

If you still aren't sure about designing the pages yourself, take a class in page layout or get a graphics student at your local community college or university to help you. Talk to the career counseling office to see about get- ting a student on an internship basis. That way, the student works for you for free and gets college credit for his/her efforts.

Examples of Kid-Friendly Layouts

The following pages show examples of kid-friendly layouts and titles from *The Lost Treasure of the Golden Sun Teacher's Guide*. "Who Said That?" and "Let's Make Fry Bread" are two-page spreads. The teacher can print them double-sided.

Who Said That?

1. Read the quotations on this worksheet. Then choose the character's name from the box below that best fits each quote and write it in the blank line under the quotation.

2. Find sentences in the *Lost Treasure* that describe the quotes and write them on a separate piece of paper.

Anny
Scout
Eric
Ben
Jim
Mr. Roanhorse
Dutch Turner
Leroy Ferguson
Dr. Sanderson
Tee-wa-nee-ka

"I am a science teacher. I think everyone is on a wild goose chase."

_____

"I really like science. I also see things that other people don't."

_____

"I could have sworn the treasure was beneath the golden sun."

_____

"I am a hataalii, a medicine man. I follow the Old Ways."

_____

"I am mysterious and have successfully guarded a secret for many years."

_____

17

CA Literature Response 2.5; Reading Comprehension 2.5
AZ Strand 1, Concept 5, Literary Response, PO 3

"I love soccer. I can lipread and use sign language. One character is my very close friend."

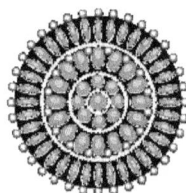

_____

"I like to tease people. I've been riding horses all my life. I also want to be an artist."

_____

"I teach at the University of Arizona and I brought the Magic Rock to the school."

_____

"Some may call me a follower, but I was just as determined to find that treasure."

_____

"I love everything about being a Girl Scout. My sister often embarrasses me."

_____

Reproducible

CA Literature Response 2.5; Reading Comprehension 2.5
AZ Strand 1, Concept 5, Literary Response, PO 3

On the Trail of the Lost Treasure

Mystery Word Search #1

Find each of the words listed below in the puzzle:

archaeologist	feather	horse	rope
Arizona	ghost	mocassins	skeleton
cave	hogan	mountain	trading post
doubloons	hoofprint	reward	treasure

G	F	M	T	R	E	A	S	U	R	E	G	R
T	S	I	G	O	L	O	E	A	H	C	R	A
R	K	Z	M	H	H	U	L	Y	O	A	E	R
A	E	H	N	D	O	E	W	T	G	V	W	I
D	L	D	I	J	R	S	G	S	A	E	A	Z
I	E	T	A	T	S	K	T	L	N	Z	R	O
N	T	B	T	F	E	A	T	H	E	R	D	N
G	O	U	N	Y	I	E	P	G	S	B	L	A
P	N	R	U	H	O	O	F	P	R	I	N	T
O	S	N	O	O	L	B	U	O	D	H	K	R
S	V	B	M	O	C	A	S	S	I	N	S	O
T	P	D	E	B	M	E	Y	J	K	F	S	P
B	C	A	V	E	M	R	C	G	D	N	P	E

Vocabulary Builder: Matching Game

Write the word from the list below in the blank beside its definition.

exasperated	episode	intuition	discomfort	premonition
vertical	rattletrap	conquistadores	glinted	encounter	distract
bore	beckon	bask	handiwork	engross

1. A rickety vehicle   _____

2. Straight up and down   _____

3. Spanish soldiers in the 16th century   _____

4. Irritated; annoyed   _____

5. An event or occurrence   _____

6. Gleamed   _____

7. Uneasiness   _____

8. Knowing of an event beforehand   _____

9. Disturb; confuse   _____

10. Go through   _____

11. Warm oneself pleasantly   _____

12. To signal with the head or hand   _____

13. Perceptions based on feelings   _____

14. Result of a person's actions   _____

15. Take up all the attention of   _____

16. Meeting   _____

CA Reading 1.0; Reading Comprehension 2.3
AZ Reading, Strand 1, Concept 4, PO 1-2

Let's Make Fry Bread

Parental or teacher supervision recommended

Ingredients

3 cups of unbleached white flour
1 cup of masa corn flour (not cornmeal)
3 tablespoons of sugar
1/2 teaspoon of salt
2 teaspoons of baking powder
1 cup of warm water
1 cup of shortening

Materials Needed

- deep, heavy pan or wok
- medium-sized bowl
- paper towels
- rolling pin
- tongs
- plate

Instructions for Cooking

1. Fill your wok or pan with 2 inches of shortening and heat over medium to medium-high heat.

2. Meanwhile, combine the dry ingredients in a bowl.

3. Make a well in the center and stir in the water. Mix to form a dough and knead briefly. The dough should be soft but not sticky. Add a little more flour or water, if necessary.

4. Cut the dough into 8 equal pieces.

5. Using your hands or the rolling pin, flatten one piece into a thin disc about 5 inches in diameter and less than 1/4 inch thick.

6. Cut a circle in the center of the bread and test the oil temperature by dropping the cut-out piece into the oil. The oil should sizzle quietly and the piece of dough should begin to change color.

   If it burns or sizzles fiercely, the temperature is too high; adjust it accordingly.

CA Mathematical Reasoning 2.6

R, ELL

7. Using the tongs, slide the bread into the oil (the oil will sizzle and bubble up through the hole in the middle) and cook until golden on the bottom, about 2 to 3 minutes.

Courtesy of the Oklahoma Historical Society

8. Using the tongs, turn the bread over, taking care not to splash yourself with oil, and cook until golden, approximately 1 1/2 to 2 1/2 more minutes.

9. As the bread cooks, shape the next piece and cut or punch a hole in the center of the dough.

10. Place the cooked bread on a plate lined with paper towels to drain while you prepare and cook the remaining breads.

To Serve

Serve warm plain or topped with powdered sugar, honey, jam, or cinnamon. For a Mexican flair, try it with beans, cheese, lettuce, tomatoes, and taco sauce.

Makes 8 servings.

The All-Important Answer Key

Including an answer key is critical so that teachers have ready access to the correct responses without having to take time to research them. The answer key should be the last page of the teacher's guide.

Answer Key

Page

6-7 *Story Quiz:* 1) Navajo Nation, Arizona; 2) Spanish gold doubloons and jewels; 3) A pictograph; 4) A vision of a fire and a headband; 5) Scout is embarrassed by Anny's strange behavior; 6) Anny is crazy; she's a liar; she has an overactive imagination; 7) To psychologists and other doctors to see what is wrong with her; 8) Using sign language; 9) Anny fears that they are losing their closeness; 10) Because he said he thought the treasure was beneath the golden sun; 11) He could lipread what they said; 12) Because it rhymes in English; 13) At Mr. Roanhorse's hogan; 14) To protect her from evil spirits; 15) When Mr. Roanhorse tells her he sees things, too, and that what she is seeing is real; 16) That he was guarding the treasure; 17) Anny learns to trust her intuition; Scout, Jim, and Ben finally believe in Anny's abilities; Jim learns to believe in the Old Ways again; Anny, Eric, and Ben realize the value of Scout's outdoor skills. *Finding the Theme:* 1) D; 2) Answers will vary.

8-9 Top - Jim; center left - Dutch Turner; center right - Anny; bottom left - Mr. Roanhorse; bottom right: Tee-wa-nee-ka; top left - Scout; top right - Ben; center - Dr. Sanderson; bottom left - Leroy Ferguson; bottom right - Scout.

10 See solution to the right.

11 1) rattletrap; 2) vertical; 3) conquistadores; 4) exasperated; 5) episode; 6) glinted; 7) discomfort; 8) premonition; 9) distract; 10) bore; 11) bask; 12) beckon; 13) intuition; 14) handiwork; 15) engross; 16) encounter.

12 *What Happened When?:* 1) 7; 2) 4; 3) 8; 4) 9; 5) 1; 6) 5; 7) 10; 8) 2; 9) 3; 10) 6. *True-False:* 1) F; 2) F; 3) F; 4) T; 5) F; 6) F.

13 Answers will vary.

17 1-4) Answers will vary; 5) Gallup; 6) New Mexico.

23 1) B; 2) J; 3) G; 4) A; 5) L; 6) D; 7) H; 8) E; 9) I; 10) F; 11) K; 12) C.

25 See solution to the right.

31 1) Millions of years ago, the trees in the forest became waterlogged, and over thousands of years, the minerals turned the wood into stone; 2) 1539; the Spanish explorers; the Anasazi and the early Navajos; 3) 5,000 feet deep; 277 miles long, and up to 18 miles wide; it was formed by the Colorado River and 500,000 years of erosion; 4) 1912.
5) To study Mars; 6) Painted Desert;
7) To use their language as a code;
8) Dinétah, or the Navajo Nation; 9) In clans.

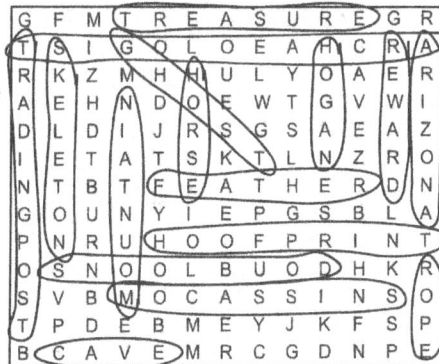
Mystery Word Search 1 Solution

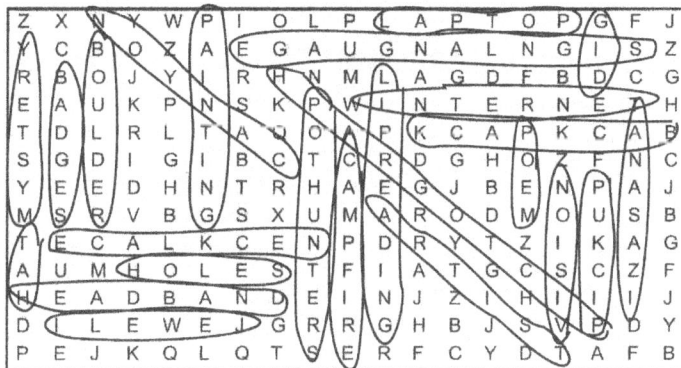
Mystery Word Search 2 Solution

32

Hiring a Book Cover Designer

Even though the old saying goes, "You can't judge a book by its cover," that's just what buyers do. If a cover isn't appealing, the consumers will not be attracted to it enough to look inside. The design is everything. You might think that if you are producing a PDF that cover design isn't important or not necessary, but this is an erroneous view. The front of your book is what is displayed on any website selling it, and it's what will attract your customers. For this reason, hiring an experienced cover designer is critical. Any money you spend on the teacher's guide should be concentrated here. Next to writing a great book, this is the smartest investment you can make. You'll need a JPG of the front for use in your marketing and on your website and in the file.

Study the Covers of Other Guides

Examine the covers of the teacher's guides in the bookstores. Many of them include a picture of the book cover they accompany. Then the teacher's guide and the book look like a set. Also include the grade level(s) for which the guide is aimed.

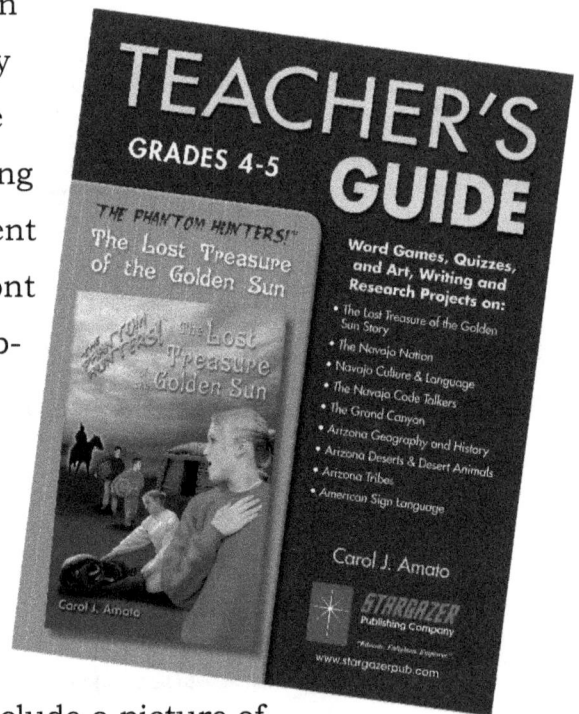

Where to Find a Cover Designer

A great resource for designers is the Independent Book Publishers' Association (www.ibpa-online.org). Go to the Vendors Resources link and submit a bid for your job. You will get responses from many designers, and you can choose from there.

In addition, check with your local university to see if any upper-division or graduate students who have designed book covers. You can also check the classifieds in *Writers' Digest*. Another great way to go is www.fiverr.com. You can get the cover design for a very low cost, but bear in mind that these vendors are usually overseas.

I highly recommend the cover designer I use (who designed the cover of this book), Michael Wheary. His website is **www.calypsoconcepts.com** and you can reach him at **mdwheary@calypsoconcepts .com**

How to Create a PDF

Once your cover and pages are designed, you're sure no changes need to be made, and you're selling your teacher's guide on your own website, you're ready to create your PDF (portable data file). You don't want to post a Word file or any other format that the buyer can change. A PDF file is hardwired; that is, it can't be altered by the average person. More sophisticated users may have programs that allow PDFs to be edited, but more often than not, this isn't an issue.

If you already have a program that creates PDF files, great! If you don't, download the free version of PDF995 from www.pdf995.com/download.html. In the right column, click the Alternate Download (free converter), Version 1.5. Install the program.

To create a PDF using PDF995, follow these steps:

1. Click File, Print. The printer dialog box will display.
2. Click the triangle next to the field that shows the current printer. The list of available printers will show up.
3. Select PDF995.
4. Click Print. The file will automatically convert to a PDF.
5. A dialog box will pop up asking for the file name and the location where you want to save it.
6. Name and save your file.

The Bottom Line

Enhancing your children's book with a teacher's guide is a terrific way to make it more saleable to the school and home-school markets. While it will take thought, creativity, and time to develop the appropriate activities, making that effort will be well worth it.

About the Author

Carol J. Amato knew she wanted to be a writer in the fourth grade. She has published twenty-nine books, around 200 articles, and two short stories. Among her memorable books for middle-graders are the critically acclaimed *Breakthroughs in Science* series (*The Earth*, *The Human Body*, *Inventions*, and *Astronomy*), *50 Nifty Science Fair Projects*, the *Super Science Project Book*, *50 More Nifty Science Fair Projects*, and the exciting mystery series *The Phantom Hunters* (#1: *The Lost Treasure of the Golden Sun*, and #2: *The Secret of Blackhurst Manor*). She is a guest speaker and has appeared on television, radio shows, and podcasts.

The Phantom Hunters takes readers to different cultures. *The Lost Treasure of the Golden Sun* takes place on the Navajo Nation and *The Secret of Blackhurst Manor* is set in Lincolnshire, England. Readers learn about the cultures and history at the same time they are reading a fast-paced mystery. Each book has an accompanying teacher's guide.

Her other recent titles include *How to Start and Run a Writers' Critique Group*, *Maximize Your Competitive Edge*, and *Running a Writers' Critique Group in Your Classroom*.

Ms. Amato has a B. A. in Spanish and French from the University of Portland (Oregon), and an M. A. in Cultural Anthropology from California State University, Fullerton.

She is a member of the Writer's Club of Whittier, a writers' workshop and the Independent Writers of Southern California (IWOSC). For three years, she served as president of the Professional Writers of Orange County (PWOC). She is listed in *Who's Who in America*, *Who's Who of American Women*, *Who's Who in the West*, *Who's Who in Orange County*, and *the World Who's Who of Women*.

Other Books by Carol J. Amato

FORERUNNER   Sept 2020
Stargazer Publishing Company, Corona, California

THE PHANTOM HUNTERS: THE SECRET OF BLACKHURST MANOR   Sept 2020
TEACHER'S GUIDE
Stargazer Publishing Company, Corona, California

THE WORLD'S EASIEST GUIDE TO USING THE APA, 6th Edition   July 2020
Stargazer Publishing Company, Corona, California

THE WORLD'S EASIEST GUIDE TO USING THE MLA, 2nd Edition   July 2020
Stargazer Publishing Company, Corona, California

THE PHANTOM HUNTERS: THE SECRET OF BLACKHURST MANOR   Apr 2019
Stargazer Publishing Company, Corona, California

MAXIMIZE YOUR COMPETITIVE EDGE: 17 SECRETS TO MAKE YOUR SMALL   Jan 2015
BUSINESS LOOK LIKE A FORTUNE 500 COMPANY
Stargazer Publishing Company, Corona, California

THE 5 BIGGEST MISTAKES SELF-PUBLISHERS MAKE AND HOW TO AVOID THEM   Aug 2011
Stargazer Publishing Company, Corona, California (Special Report)

WRITING COOL SHORT STORIES   May 2009
Stargazer Publishing Company, Corona, California

THE WORLD'S EASIEST GUIDE TO USING THE APA, 4th Edition   Jan 2009
Stargazer Publishing Company, Corona, California

RUNNING A WRITERS' CRITIQUE GROUP IN YOUR CLASSROOM   Nov 2007
Stargazer Publishing Company, Corona, California

HOW TO START AND RUN A WRITERS' CRITIQUE GROUP   May 2006
Stargazer Publishing Company, Corona, California

THE PHANTOM HUNTERS: THE LOST TREASURE OF THE GOLDEN SUN   Feb 2006
TEACHER'S GUIDE
Stargazer Publishing Company, Corona, California

THE PHANTOM HUNTERS!™: THE LOST TREASURE OF THE GOLDEN SUN   Sept 2005
Stargazer Publishing Company, Corona, California

ERSISTENCE IS POWER! A REAL-WORLD GUIDE FOR THE NEWLY DISABLED   Oct 2004
EMPLOYEE
Stargazer Publishing Company, Corona, California

THE WORLD'S EASIEST GUIDE TO USING THE APA, 3rd Edition   Sept 2002
Stargazer Publishing Company, Corona, California

THE WORLD'S EASIEST GUIDE TO USING THE APA, 2nd Edition   Nov 1998
Stargazer Publishing Company, Westminster, California

THE WORLD'S EASIEST GUIDE TO USING THE MLA   May 1999
Stargazer Publishing Company, Westminster, California

Other Books by Carol J. Amato, Continued

THE WORLD'S EASIEST GUIDE TO USING THE APA, 2nd Edition   Nov 1998
Stargazer Publishing Company, Westminster, California

THE EARTH   Nov 1995
Teacher Created Materials, Westminster, California

CREEPY CRAWLIES   Nov 1995
Teacher Created Materials, Westminster, California

THE WORLD'S EASIEST GUIDE TO USING THE APA   Aug 1995
Stargazer Publishing Company, Westminster, California

50 NIFTY SUPER SCIENCE FAIR PROJECTS   May 1995
RGA-Lowell House, Los Angeles, California

SUPER SCIENCE FAIR PROJECTS   Aug 1994
RGA-Lowell House, Los Angeles, California

50 NIFTY SCIENCE FAIR PROJECTS   Dec 1992
RGA-Lowell House, Los Angeles, California (for Scholastic)

INSIDE OUT: MODERN TECHNOLOGY EXPLAINED   Fall 1992
Smithmark Publishing Co., New York

BREAKTHROUGHS in SCIENCE: THE EARTH   Fall 1992
Smithmark Publishing Co., New York

BREAKTHROUGHS in SCIENCE: ASTRONOMY   Fall 1992
Smithmark Publishing Co., New York

BREAKTHROUGHS in SCIENCE: THE HUMAN BODY   Spring 1992
Smithmark Publishing Co., New York

BREAKTHROUGHS in SCIENCE: INVENTIONS   Spring 1992
Smithmark Publishing Co., New York

OUR CURRENT CULTURAL CRISIS   1986
California State University Press, Fullerton, California

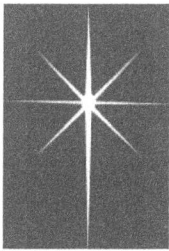

STARGAZER
Publishing Company

"Educate, Enlighten, Empower"

Mystery adventure series!

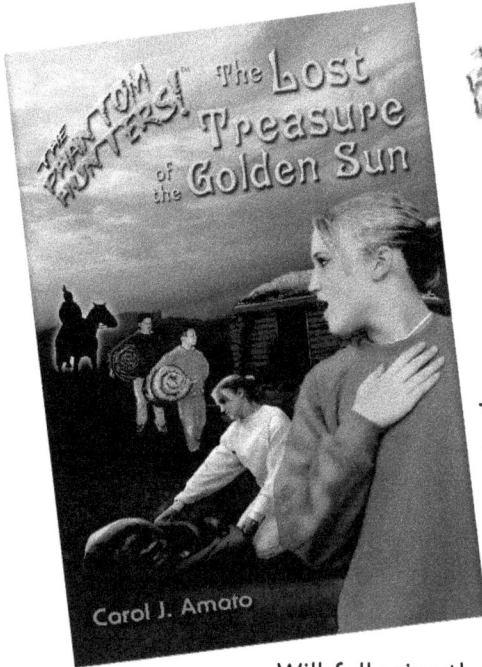

#1 The Lost Treasure of the Golden Sun
by Carol J. Amato

Ages 8-12

978-1-933277-01-1
5.5" x 8.5"   176 pages
Hardcover, $15.95
Softcover, $9.95

Twelve-year-old Anny Bradford is different, very different. She sees things that other people don't. When she sees a startling vision of a warrior on a trip to the Navajo Nation, once again, her twin sister, Scout, and their Navajo friend, Ben Lapahie, don't believe her. Only one person does: her other close friend, Eric Larson. He knows what it's like to be misunderstood. He's deaf. Anny senses her vision has something to do with lost treasure, a mysterious fire, and two visiting archaeologists. Will following the clues lead them to a treasure or to an untimely end?

"Reminiscent of Nancy Drew titles, this mystery moves quickly.... Readers learn about Native American culture and tradition as they are carried along by the adventure."

- School Library Journal

Teacher's Guide
for Grades 4-5

978-1-933277-06-6
8.5" x 11"   32 pages
Softcover $12.95

The Lost Treasure of the Golden Sun helps young readers understand differences. Through *The Phantom Hunters!* characters, kids will experience foreign cultures and learn tolerance and respect for others and trust in one's own judgment.

Fully compliant with California Department of Education standards for Grade 5 and Arizona Department of Education Standards for Grade 4, this teacher's guide is a companion to *The Lost Treasure of the Golden Sun*. It contains word games, quizzes, and art, writing, and research projects on *The Lost Treasure of the Golden Sun* story; the Navajo Nation; Navajo culture and language; the Navajo Code Talkers; the Grand Canyon; Arizona geography, history and tribes; Arizona deserts and desert animals; and American Sign Language. Full of reproducibles, this teacher's guide's activities and lessons plans will get kids thinking, talking, writing, understanding—and signing!

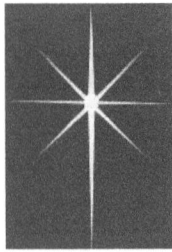

STARGAZER
Publishing Company

"Educate, Enligh ten, Empower"

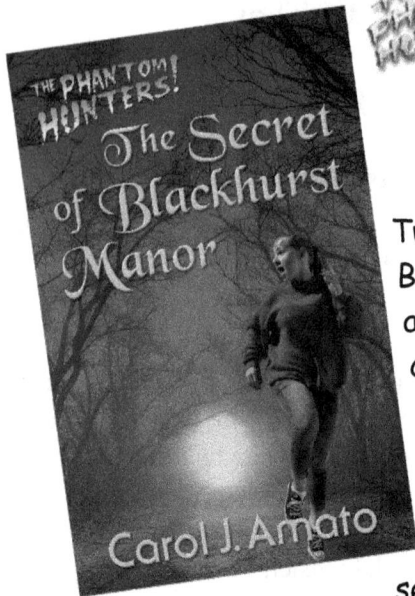

THE PHANTOM HUNTERS!

#2 The Secret of Blackhurst Manor

978-1933277028
5.5" x 8.5"   230 pages
Softcover, $9.95

978-1933277035
Kindle $2.95

Twelve-year-old Anny Bradford is stunned when she inherits Blackhurst Manor in England. She, her twin sister Scout, and their family travel there from California only to discover the enormous mansion in ruins.

Why would Grandpa have left her this wreck?

And Great-aunt Beatrice, who supposedly lives in the manor, has vanished without a trace.

When a strange teenaged boy and a man in a dark-green sedan follow her and her family from one place to another as they tour the ancient city of Lincoln, she once again gets that creepy feeling. And who are the Roman soldiers roaming Lincoln Castle grounds? Are they park characters or something more sinister?

Someone--or something--clearly doesn't want Anny and her family near Black-hurst Manor, and she is determined to find out why.

Teacher's Guide
for Grades 6

978-1933277134
8.5" x 11"   32 pages
Softcover $4.95

Fully compliant with California Department of Education standards for Grade 6, this teacher's guide is a companion to *The Secret of Blackhurst Manor*. It contains word games, quizzes, and art, writing, and research projects on *The Secret of Blackhurst Manor* story; the Romans in Britain; Roman culture and language; Julius Caesar; the City of Lincoln; Lincoln Castle; Lincoln Cathedral; Magna Carta; British culture, geography, and history; and British vs. American English. Full of reproducibles, this teacher's guide's activities and lessons plans will get kids thinking, talking, writing, and understanding.

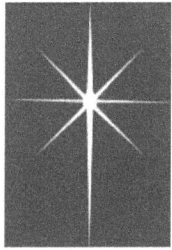

STARGAZER
Publishing Company

"Educate, Enlighten, Empower"

978-1933277202
8.5" x 11"   28 pages
Softcover, $4.95

Running a Writers' Critique Group in Your Classroom

by Carol J. Amato

Professional writers have used critique groups for years.

What is a critique group?

It is a meeting of writers who read and comment on one another's work before it goes to an editor. The feedback provides them with hundreds of tips regarding plot, characterization, dialogue, and theme in fiction; article leads and closes; and structure for nonfiction books. . Without this feedback, members claim their manuscripts may not have sold as soon as they did and would have needed much more editing.

Many students have problems writing clearly. Why not use the critique group format in the classroom setting to allow them to provide feedback on one another's work before the assignments get turned in for a grade?

In critique groups, members learn as much from hearing the feedback of others' manuscripts as they do from hearing comments about their own. Students are no different. This is the big benefit to running such a group in your classroom: Rather than creating their assignments alone in a vacuum, students can gain knowledge from one another. They will learn more about the writing process; how to spot grammar, punctuation, and spelling errors; and how to clearly express their thoughts. This can take the frustration factor out of preparing assignments. It also can result in their getting higher grades through the submission of far better products than they could have produced otherwise. In addition, the more polished documents will be easier for you to grade.

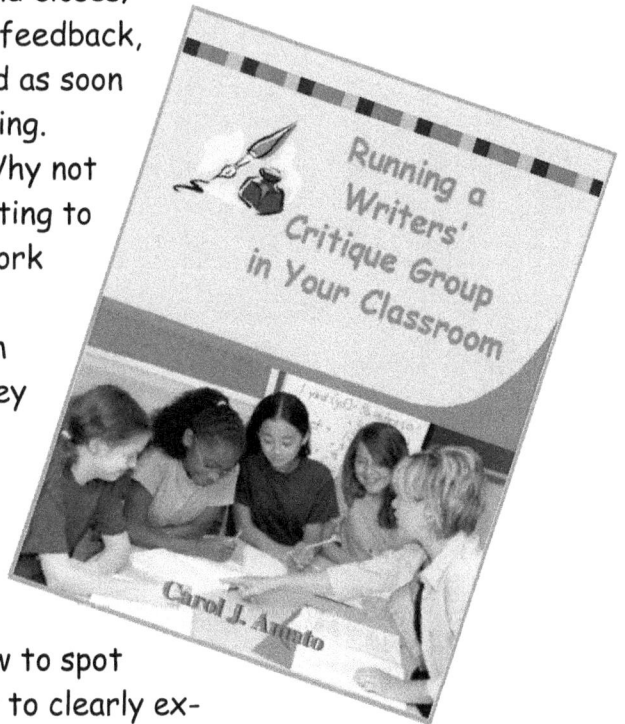

Acknowledgements

My heartfelt thanks to my trusted critique group colleagues, whose help and advice have been invaluable: Steve Attkisson, Mandy Baker, Anita Burns, Molly Dillon, Maria De Maci, Alanna Heck, Lynn Kelley, David Lintner, C. Sonberg Larsen, Judith L. McAllister, Kathy Sant, Maria Cisneros Toth, and Amy Walterman.